THE EXCELLENCE BOOK

50 WAYS TO FULFILL YOUR POTENTIAL IN WORK AND LIFE

KEVIN DUNCAN
ROSIE DUNCAN

T0002364

PRAISE FOR
THE EXCELLENCE BOOK

"It's been great to work with Kevin and Rosie over the years – they're a great duo. Our team enjoy all of their books and workshops as they bring different perspectives on a huge range of subjects, across generations and genders."

CHARLEY WALSH
Senior Learning and Development Manager, TBWA/Media Arts Lab

"Wonderful, concrete, useful advice delivered in a manner that takes concision to a new level and is sure to appeal to busy executives."

EUAN SEMPLE
ex-BBC, and author of *Organizations Don't Tweet, People Do*

"No-one does 'bite-size' like Kevin. His morsels are meaty, richly flavoursome and deeply satisfying. Your intellectual taste buds will sigh with pleasure."

RICHARD SWAAB
Deputy Chairman BBDO EMEA

"Time spent reading Kevin Duncan's books is never wasted. At the very least you will be entertained and I defy you not to discover at least one nugget of wisdom to add to your chuckles."

PAULA CARTER
Director of Planning, Channel 4

Published by
LID Publishing
An imprint of LID Business Media Ltd.
LABS House, 15-19 Bloomsbury Way,
London, WC1A 2TH, UK

info@lidpublishing.com
www.lidpublishing.com

A member of:

BPR ✷
businesspublishersroundtable.com

© Kevin Duncan and Rosie Duncan, 2023
© LID Business Media Limited, 2023

Printed by Severn, Gloucester

ISBN: 978-1-911498-51-3 (hardback)
ISBN: 978-1-915951-07-6 (paperback)
ISBN: 978-1-915951-08-3 (ebook)

Cover and page design: Caroline Li

THE EXCELLENCE BOOK

50 WAYS TO FULFILL YOUR POTENTIAL IN WORK AND LIFE

KEVIN DUNCAN
ROSIE DUNCAN

MADRID | MEXICO CITY | LONDON
BUENOS AIRES | BOGOTA | SHANGHAI

FOR OTHER TITLES
IN THE SERIES...

CONCISE
ADVICE
LAB

SMALL
BOOKS:
BIG
IDEAS

CLEVER CONTENT, DYNAMIC IDEAS, PRACTICAL
SOLUTIONS AND ENGAGING VISUALS –
A CATALYST TO INSPIRE NEW WAYS OF THINKING
AND PROBLEM-SOLVING IN A COMPLEX WORLD

conciseadvicelab.com

"We are what we repeatedly do. Excellence, then, is not an act but a habit."
Will Durant, historian, after Aristotle.

Many thanks for endorsement and comment:
Chris Barez-Brown, Paula Carter, Paul Davies, Mark Earls, Jonathan Harman, Ian Mason, Greg McKeown, Marty Neumeier, Rob Norman, Euan Semple, Rory Sutherland, Richard Swaab and Charley Walsh.

And for good wishes and support:
Seth Godin, Patrick Lencioni, Daniel Levitin, Dan Pink, Ken Segall, Simon Sinek and Susan Cain.

CONTENTS

INTRODUCTION

Five years ago, in the original book introduction, I explained that with everyone so frantically busy, I had responded by writing shorter and shorter.

The idea was that, in this format, anyone can grab some inspiration in less than hour, and sometimes in less than a minute.

Since then, a lot has happened in the world, and the topic of mental health has become important for almost everyone.

The time is right to bring different perspectives to the subject, by involving my daughter Rosie who can offer views across the generations.

People often ask us where we get this stuff from.

The answer is: a little from everywhere.

We call it being a mental magpie.

You won't notice any of it if you have your head permanently buried in a screen.

The Excellence Book aims to help you be the best you can be and fulfill your potential in work and life. Anywhere. At home, at work, with your family.

It's not a competition. It's about quality.

Good luck applying these ideas, and, as ever, do let us know how you get on.

Kevin Duncan
Westminster 2023

A WORD ON ATTITUDE

Attitude is either a settled way of thinking or feeling about
something, or truculent or uncooperative behaviour.

It's your choice how you view the world.

Some people wake up angry with everything,
and carry that stress on through the day.

Others are calmer, and generally have a better time of it.

It really pays to decide what your particular attitude is.

It can transform your life.

A negative attitude gets you nowhere.

A positive attitude can get you anywhere.

Experiences help. So does listening to those of others.

You can then apply the wisdom to your own circumstances.

Here are ten suggestions to help you decide your perspective.

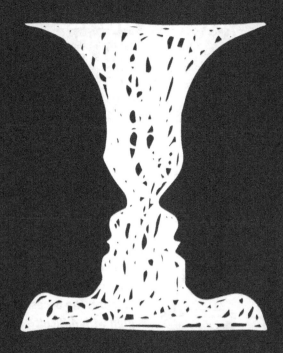

PART ONE

ATTITUDE

1.
DISENTHRALL
YOURSELF

On 1 December 1862, President Abraham Lincoln delivered his annual message to Congress. The country was in the middle of a civil war. He concluded:

"The dogmas of the quiet past are inadequate to the stormy present. The occasion is piled high with difficulty, and we must rise with the occasion. As our case is new, so we must think anew, and act anew. We must disenthrall ourselves, and then we shall save our country."

Disenthrall. It's an interesting word.

To enthrall means to capture someone's attention.

This could be good or bad, depending on what exactly is attracting your undivided attention.

To disenthrall means to discharge, free, emancipate, liberate, loosen, release, unbind, uncage, unchain or unfetter.

So, if you are obsessed with perpetually doing or seeing things in a certain way, you may first need to disenthrall yourself to stand any chance of changing your attitude.

Only then will you have a chance of seeing other possibilities.

In order to change any of our own habits and behaviours, we must first become aware of them. From this perspective, we can analyse whether that's how we would, or wouldn't, like to respond to any given situation. Next time you find yourself reacting badly, note down what happened and how you behaved. When you have some time for reflection, look at this from an outsider's perspective.

ASK YOURSELF
What are your triggers and what did you learn about yourself?

2.
YOU ARE
WHAT YOU DO

There is no point in claiming to have a certain attitude, when your actions either fail to prove it, or worse, contradict it.

As Aristotle said:
"We are what we repeatedly do."

Thinking is one thing. Doing is quite another.

Gina Miller, the businesswoman who initiated a court case against the British government challenging its authority to implement Brexit, said:

"What's the point in having a conscience if you never use it?"

The popular blogger and author Mark Manson, points this out in his unsubtly named book *The Subtle Art of Not Giving a F*ck*:

"Who you are is defined by what you're willing to struggle for."

You can rarely think your way into a new way of acting.

You need to act your way into a new way of thinking.

In other words, the action proves the thought.

Without action, it merely remains a concept and, as such, doesn't technically exist.

We know that we are happier, more productive human beings if we are working in line with our values. When things at work get tough, which inevitably happens, we know at the very least that we aren't battling with our personal principles. Company and personal values have become increasingly important over the decades. A recent Deloitte study shows that Gen Zs and millennials are even willing to turn down jobs and assignments which don't align with their values.[1]

ASK YOURSELF

What values do you live by, and how well do these align with what you do?

3.
CULTIVATE A FEISTY SPIRIT

Resilience in the face of adversity is a vital trait.

Life is not a smooth road. In fact, if it were, most of us would be bored.

As noted by Max McKeown in his book *#Now*, those confronted by extremely tricky obstacles (such as cancer) are said to have a 'feisty spirit of survivorship'.

It's a laughing-is-winning approach, and is something that can be adopted by anyone, including those facing life-threatening circumstances.

This transformative ability to make good things happen through a positive attitude is a quality you can discover in yourself.

The famous mountaineer
Edmund Hillary pointed out:
*"It is not the mountain we
conquer but ourselves."*

It's all about taking control of your attitude to life: one person's adversity is another's inspiration.

It's not easy to get back up once we've been knocked down. But if we never get back up again, we will never get anywhere. Absolutely everybody fails at some point, some more than others. It's our attitude to failure, and cultivating resilience, that allows us to strive and continue. So, when you face a setback (which you will), take some time afterwards to take stock.

ASK YOURSELF
Can you reframe the situation and find a positive that came from it?

4.
FEAR = WISDOM IN THE FACE OF DANGER

*"Fear is wisdom in the face
of danger. It's nothing to
be ashamed of."*

So said Sherlock Holmes in *The Abominable Bride*.

It's okay to be afraid. In fact, it's often beneficial.

Animals have a clearly demarcated sense of flight or fight.

And it's driven by fright. Which is a sudden intense feeling of fear.

So being scared can be extremely beneficial for survival or progress.

Not so that you are petrified into non-action.

But so that you fully appreciate the possibilities that may follow from your actions.

Harness the fear to anticipate what to do next.

Flight could allow you to fight another day.

A fight should only be considered if you are convinced you can win.

Confront the initial fear and turn it into a wise attitude.

Fear is a natural reaction to the unknown as it keeps us alert for dangers that arise from new situations. This means that every new venture will come with a healthy dollop of apprehension. We cannot get rid of fear, but we can learn to accept it. And each time you overcome it, you will learn not to be afraid of a new situation.

ASK YOURSELF
What can you do that is just out of your comfort zone?

5.
CLIMB, CONFESS, COMPLY

Student pilots are taught early in their training what to do if they get into trouble:

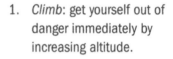

1. *Climb*: get yourself out of danger immediately by increasing altitude.

2. *Confess*: talk to the control tower and explain what the problem is.

3. *Comply*: do exactly what you are told by the air traffic controller.

Climb, confess, comply is a useful attitude when dealing with awkward circumstances.

So, next time you are out of your depth, admit it immediately, ask for help quickly, and then do exactly what it takes to resolve the situation.

Don't dig a deeper hole or paint yourself into a corner.

Climb, confess, comply.

We can predict that something, at some point, will go wrong. This is not designed to scare you, but rather to prepare you. It happens to all of us, no matter who we are. Whenever you do fail, give it your best shot not to let it define you. By sharing the issue and working through it, you aren't suffering alone.

ASK YOURSELF
When you last failed, how did you handle it, and would you do something differently next time?

6.
NO ONE ELSE IS INTERESTED

In his memoirs, *Gig: The Life and Times of a Rock-star Fantasist*, British poet Simon Armitage recalls returning to his hometown.

There, in the bargain bin of a second-hand bookshop, he found a copy of one of his own books.

It was inscribed in the front, in his own handwriting, *'To Mum and Dad'*.

Despite their son pouring his best efforts into having a book published, his parents obviously didn't consider it worth keeping.

Which just goes to show that however much you care about something, other people probably don't.

In fact, they might not even be interested.

One person's passion may be another's ambivalence.

It's up to you to decide what you feel strongly about.

But don't expect anyone else to care.

Do your parents really understand what you do for a living?

The Spotlight Effect is a psychological concept by which people overestimate how much others are focused on us. In reality, everyone's spotlight is on themselves. It's highly likely that, when you think you're being judged, your companion is busy thinking the same thing about themselves. In the kindest way, no one is giving you as much attention as you think.

ASK YOURSELF
Can you keep this in mind the next time you think you're being judged?

7.
PERFORMANCE = ABILITY MINUS INTERFERENCE

According to Tim Gallwey, author of *The Inner Game of Tennis*, performance is ability minus interference.

Ability means you can get the job done skillfully.

But we all know that even the best have bad days.

Being worried or distracted debilitates your ability to concentrate and do things well.

So, on a personal level, if you want to do something well, remove all the distractions you can so you can get on and do your best.

Bosses and whole companies can learn from this too.

If an individual, or even an entire department, is to do something well, then they need to be allowed to get on with it.

Don't interfere. It reduces effective performance.

Thanks to mobile phones, it is possible for people to contact us, and 'interfere' with us, every second of the day. We have become *always on*. According to a 2017 University of California study, every time we are distracted it takes 23 minutes and 15 seconds to get back to what we were working on.[2] This means that if we are distracted 4 times an hour, we will not get anything done all day. It's easy to see how this would impede our performance. So, we need to limit this interference.

ASK YOURSELF
What interferes with you – your phone, your thoughts – and what can you do to put these on pause?

BE A
POSSIBILIST

Pessimists look smart because they see problems everywhere.

They even like it when things go wrong because it proves they were right to be pessimistic.

Optimists look stupid because they think everything can be done.

It is easy for cynics to laugh at their apparently blind enthusiasm.

Possibilists can strike a balance between the two.

What's the best possible thing we could do here?

In geography circles, possibilism proposes that culture and human agency determine human behaviour rather than the environment (as environmental determinists would have us believe).

Possibilists believe they can find an intelligent way through – staying positive while remaining pragmatic.

Most things work out fine, so let's start by assuming that they will.

As individuals, we can't be optimistic all the time. If we are continuously positive and therefore ignore reality – which includes the bad parts - we are suppressing important parts of ourselves that are there for a reason. Fear and worry are designed to protect us. This concept is called *spiritual bypassing*; a "tendency to use spiritual ideas and practices to sidestep or avoid facing unresolved emotional issues, psychological wounds, and unfinished developmental tasks." The term was introduced in the mid 1980s by John Welwood, a Buddhist teacher and psychotherapist.

ASK YOURSELF
Are you using positivity and optimism to avoid difficult situations?

9.
BE AN
ESSENTIALIST

In his book *Essentialism*, Greg McKeown espouses the disciplined pursuit of less.

The non-essentialist is all things to all people, pursues everything in an undisciplined way, and lives a life that does not satisfy.

He or she thinks that almost everything is essential.

The essentialist does less but better, creating a life that really matters.

He or she thinks that almost everything is non-essential.

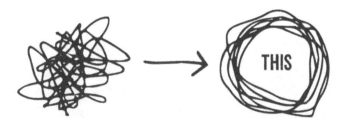

If it isn't a clear yes, then it's a clear no.

Instead of doing many things half-heartedly, do one or two things properly.

It takes the same amount of energy, but is much more fulfilling.

Concentrate only on what is essential.

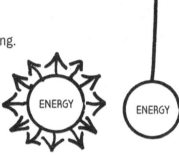

This concept works just as well for the things that we own. James Wallman's book *Stuffocation* explores how we are 'stuffocating' with all the things that we have. It's not stuff that makes us happy, it's memories and experiences. Clutter in the home is clutter in the mind. Marie Kondo's technique asks this question of every item: does it bring you joy, or does it have a practical use? If it doesn't do either, it needs to go.[3]

ASK YOURSELF
Can you declutter your life by recycling or giving away things that you no longer need?

10.
SIT AND BE

Blaise Pascal, the French mathematician, said:
"All of man's misery comes from his incapacity to sit alone in an empty quiet room."

We are useless at doing nothing, but, when we rush into things, we usually cause trouble for ourselves, and for others.

In his book *An Optimist's Tour of the Future*, Mark Stevenson relates a story told by Tim Langley, director of charcoal manufacturer Carbonscape.

An elderly German businessman and his wife hired Tim and his boat to go looking for dolphins.

There were none to be found, but they kept pushing Tim to keep looking.

Eventually after two hours, Tim asked: *"Do you want to continue looking, or do you just want to sit and be?"*

Such an idea had never occurred to the German.

In order to determine a decent attitude, we need to pause and think properly.

Sometimes we just need to sit and be.

We cannot 'do' all the time. Excess productivity leads to burnout – which, in turn, forces us to do nothing as we are no longer capable. In order to have the energy to 'do' things well, we need to have rested. Resting brings us down from a doing, adrenal, fight-or-flight state into a calming, rest-and-digest state. In this state we get better sleep, which means our cells regenerate properly, and prepare us better for the next day. Recharging is therefore essential to being a healthy human being.

ASK YOURSELF
What time can you block out to just sit, be, and recharge?

HOW TO CULTIVATE A HEALTHY MENTALITY

1. Change the way you normally do things

2. Concentrate hard on what you actually do

3. Cultivate a feisty spirit

4. Confront fear and turn it into opportunity

5. Confess when something goes wrong, then seek advice

6. Assume no one else cares and become resilient in your own right

7. Remove distractions and interference to improve your performance

8. Clarify what is truly possible

9. Become an essentialist

10. Be comfortable to just sit and be

PLEDGES

Things you are going to do differently based on the ideas in this section

1. _____

_____

_____

2. _____

_____

_____

3. _____

_____

_____

A WORD ON APPROACH

We have thought about attitude.

Now let's look at approach.

What's the difference?

Attitude is how you choose to think.

Approach is what you then do.

Your approach is the way you choose to deal with
a problem or situation.

It can also mean that you are coming near, or nearer,
to someone or something in distance or in time.

It's time for action or reaction.

So that's either making a proposal or request, or handling one.

It's hard to behave as you truly want without having thought
about what your approach is going to be.

It's time to put your attitude into practice,
and have it tested by events.

PART TWO

APPROACH

1.
EFFORT CREATES OPPORTUNITY

"Opportunity is missed by most people because it is dressed in overalls and looks like work."
The American inventor Thomas Edison said that.

He was also the man behind:

"I have not failed. I've just found 10,000 ways that won't work."

And:

"Genius is one per cent inspiration and ninety-nine per cent perspiration."

People love the idea of being successful. Of achievement.

But often they are simply in love with the idea of the result.

They want the reward, but in truth they just aren't prepared to put in the work to get there.

To create opportunities and achieve more of what you want, your approach needs to involve applied effort.

So, how can we make what we want more achievable? First, we need to *know* what we want. Then, we need to work out the small and manageable steps that will get us there, taking a lofty - and potentially overwhelming - goal and breaking it down into clear, bite-size tasks. Each time we take another step towards our goal by fulfilling a task, we are motivating ourselves through that achievement. It becomes a self-motivating cycle.

ASK YOURSELF
What is your goal? What steps will get you there?

2.
LOSING YOUR ALBEDO

Albedo is the proportion of the light or radiation reflected by a surface, typically that of a planet such as earth.

Ice, especially with snow on top of it, has a high albedo, so most sunlight hitting the surface bounces back towards space.

The more snow, the more reflection.

The albedo effect, therefore, becomes a self-reinforcing phenomenon.

It can be true of our approach too.

The more you behave in a certain way, the more entrenched in that behaviour you become.

This has been described as self-protecting activity.

You've probably heard
the Einstein quote:
**"Insanity is doing the same
thing over and over again and
expecting different results."**

If it's not working, change your approach.

The *Low Mood Loop*[4] is a self-fulfilling cycle that perpetuates low energy behaviours and negative thoughts. Low mood gives you the urge to act in unproductive and unhealthy ways. We tend not to exercise, to eat badly, to isolate. This in turn keeps us in a low mood state. The way out of this is to fake positivity until it works. We can do this by influencing our environment, eating well, and 'forcing' exercise or movement. Researchers have found that even a fake smile can "trick" your brain into thinking you're happy.

ASK YOURSELF
How can you break the cycle?

3.
BETTER
AND CHEAPER

Lord Ernest Rutherford was a British physicist who became known as the father of nuclear physics. He uttered these immortal words:
"We have no money so we will have to think."

It has become fashionable to say, and probably believe, that so-called 'big ideas' require big budgets.

This is nonsense.

An idea is an idea. And if it's good enough, then it's good enough.

In fact, the better the idea, the lower the price tag.

Perversely, bad ideas cost the same as good ones.

Your approach should be to reduce emphasis on resources, and concentrate on the thought.

That way, things could be both better *and* cheaper.

Constraints are a helpful thing. To start working on a project, we need a brief. And the tighter the brief, the more focused the answer will be. Morgan & Barden's book *A Beautiful Constraint* explains how constraints can lead to greater originality and ingenuity. Limitation can be incredibly powerful for creativity as it forces us to work with the tools that we have. If we're stuck, it's our approach that needs to change.

ASK YOURSELF
How can you approach a problem with a new perspective?

KEEP THE BEST, BIN THE REST

We live in an age of too many ideas.

People always say they are looking for ideas.

What they really mean is that they need a smart idea that is practicable.

Most ideas fall into two categories:

1. Not that exciting.
2. Interesting, but unrealistic to implement.

A good idea is both exciting and doable.

But we have too many of those too.

St. Jerome was a very brainy priest, theologian and historian who lived around the year 400 and translated the bible into Latin. His personal mantra was:

"Good, better, best
Never let it rest
'Til your good is better
And your better is best."

In other words, keep only the best, and bin the rest.

It's the only way to keep quality at its highest level.

By focusing on fewer tasks we give each of them more energy, time and effort. This will naturally produce better results. As well as better results, you will become more knowledgeable on each subject you concentrate on. This will lead to consistently better ideas. But to do this, we need to give ourselves the time and space to focus. This means cutting unnecessary things from our daily tasks or delegating them to someone else.

ASK YOURSELF

Look at your to do list. What can you get rid of or delegate so that you have a clear focus?

5.
A DIFFERENT
TYPE OF LEARNING

In a 2014 Princeton and UCLA study, researchers found that students who took notes on their laptops took twice as many notes as those who took them by hand.

Sounds impressive.

But when they tested them, the longhand note takers did twice as well.

Every time they repeated it, the same thing happened.

Writing forces the listener to process the information properly, even if interpreting it only for their own note taking purposes.

Whereas the laptop typists are like court stenographers on autopilot.

So when we encounter new information and want to learn from it, we need to force ourselves to *do something* with it.

Describe it to someone else.

Try out a suggested approach. See what happens.

Learn, refine and go again.

Our computers are the ultimate portal to self-distraction. One minute we're researching, the next we're responding to an email. Add mass distraction to screen fatigue, and we create a good argument for stepping away from our laptops. Working through things with pen and paper gives us a better chance to focus and cultivate our thoughts before expressing them digitally. The next time you need to think on a problem, step away from the screen.

ASK YOURSELF
Which project can you practice this on?

TRY EVERYTHING ONCE

"Try everything once except incest and folk dancing."

This was the advice of the famous conductor Sir Thomas Beecham.

One of these activities is illegal, the other merely polarizing.

As long as it's legal, it's worth investigating everything.

You could take someone else's word for it.

Or you could try it yourself.

It depends on how much you trust the source, and how vicariously you wish to live.

Nothing really beats personal exposure to something.

If you don't enjoy it, don't do it again.

Inquisitiveness is good. But masochism isn't.

Everyone makes mistakes, and when you have made enough, they call it experience.

Paulo Coelho, the Brazilian novelist, advises:

"Be brave. Take risks. Nothing can substitute experience."

So make your approach investigative.

A 2019 study reported in Forbes claims that '*A staggering 74 percent of Americans prioritize experiences over products.*'[5] Experiences have become valued far above material possessions with customers choosing holidays over owning the latest car. Experiences offer us a long-lasting memory that we share with others. They allow us to create deeper bonds and a sense of community, making us happier all in all than the instant and short-lived dopamine hit that we get from shopping.

ASK YOURSELF
What have you always wanted to try?

7.
DON'T FORCE FIT

Jerry Seinfeld, the American comedian, actor and director once wryly observed:
"It's amazing that the amount of news that happens in the world every day always just exactly fits the newspaper."

And of course it doesn't.

And yet we often hang on to rigid and inflexible constructs to organize what we see and do.

You don't chop the legs off a rabbit to fit it in the hutch.

So you don't always have to force fit things into a set format or template.

It can feel counterintuitive, because we are hardwired to find shape where often there is none.

Like seeing shapes in clouds.

Or believing a mass of data has some kind of pattern.

Sometimes it just doesn't.

And no structured approach can help with that.

We have to allow for the grey areas in life, and to find comfort in them. Black and white thinking is a psychological construct whereby if you aren't everything, it means that you are nothing. If you haven't succeeded, then you have failed. If you aren't a brilliant swimmer, it means you must be an awful one. It doesn't allow for any other variations to sit in between. This thinking only allows for extremes, can leave us feeling inadequate, and is hard to negotiate.

ASK YOURSELF
Do you fall into the category of a black and white thinker?

8.
THE SPRINGBOARD
OF SOLITUDE

According to Agnes Martin, the American abstract painter:

"The best things in life happen when you're alone."

Working together is great, but the principle of collaboration is often abused.

Many executives get a lot more done at home than in the office.

That's because they have uninterrupted time to think and do.

There's little worse than someone dumping all their random thoughts on you, hoping you will sort out their thinking for them.

It is everyone's responsibility to think as hard as possible about an issue before burdening someone else with half-baked ideas.

Solitude enables you to get your thoughts together.

So use thoughtful time alone as a springboard for a better approach.

As the guitarist and singer Chrissie Hynde points out: **"Being alone is underrated."**

Solitude is necessary to recover and regroup. In Judith Orloff's *The Empath's Survival Guide*, she explains that taking time away from other people is essential to rebalance your own energy, especially for empaths, who are on the more sensitive end of the spectrum. Being alone will help us recharge, but is also a sign of contentment, since being comfortable in our own skin is the ultimate self-compliment.

ASK YOURSELF
When can you set aside some alone time?

9.
PROBLEM OWNER, NOT PROBLEM MOANER

Okay, so it's a word play, but it works.

Anyone can raise their eyeballs to the heavens and say:

"Well this is a big problem, isn't it?"

These people are no help.

Someone needs to address the issue, taking responsibility, and making suggestions about how to improve matters.

Otherwise we will all just sit around nodding sagely and confirming that there is, indeed, a problem.

And if there is a problem, then that must be the worst kind of inertia to have.

Grab it by the scruff of the neck, work through some possible approaches, and try something.

Become a problem owner, not a problem moaner.

How we tackle problems is a good indicator as to how we tackle life. Do you ignore the problem, hoping it will go away? Do you highlight the problem, but let it hang in the air, unresolved? Both have their issues. Ignoring the problem won't mean it magically disappears. By highlighting it, we may feel very clever for spotting it, but we are creating disruption without a solution. To be a constructive member of any community, we need to understand the problem *and* work out how to solve it. You will be respected for your realistic and helpful approach.

ASK YOURSELF
How do you tackle problems?

10.
ROUTINE = DEATH

If you keep doing the same old thing, then you'll just be doing, well, the same old thing.

Such consistency may be admirable in some spheres, but in most instances you will want to progress.

Most humans become bored easily.

So if things have become repetitive, it may be time to make some changes.

Alter the pattern.

Take some measured risks.

Live a little.

As Paulo Coelho, the Brazilian novelist, observes:

"If you think adventure is dangerous, try routine; it is lethal."

Slow atrophy is no future for anyone pursuing excellence.

Seek variety.

Be inquisitive. Be industrious. Aim for top quality.

Think hard. Experiment.

Learn. Refine your approach.

Neophilia is the desire to experience new things. Research has shown that it is a precursor to a healthier and happier life, because by experiencing something new our brain is stimulated and gives us a hit of dopamine, creating a rush of excitement. As humans we are naturally curious creatures, and by indulging in the new we are creating fresh neural pathways in our brains, allowing us to handle any novel situation.

ASK YOURSELF
What curiosity could you explore?

HOW TO
CULTIVATE A HEALTHY
MENTALITY

1. Put the effort in to create opportunity

2. Remove self-protecting activities

3. Concentrate on better ideas rather than big budgets

4. Improve quality by ditching ideas that are good, but not great

5. Use a pen, not a laptop

6. Try everything once, within reason

7. Don't force fit things unnecessarily

8. Use solitude as productive thinking time

9. Own problems, don't moan about them

10. Break your routine sometimes

PLEDGES

Things you are going to do differently based on the ideas in this section

1. _____

_____

_____

2. _____

_____

_____

3. _____

_____

_____

A WORD ON TIMING

You have worked out your attitude and decided on your approach.

So when exactly are you going to act?

This could prove crucial.

According to the *Collins Dictionary*, time is:

"The continuous passage of existence in which events pass from a state of potentiality in the future, through the present, to a state of finality in the past."

So that's all clear then.

One thing is for sure.

We have real trouble dealing with it.

The unemployed person has too much time on their hands, and the stressed executive hasn't got enough of it.

Your view of time can make a big difference, so let's try to get a grip on how time works.

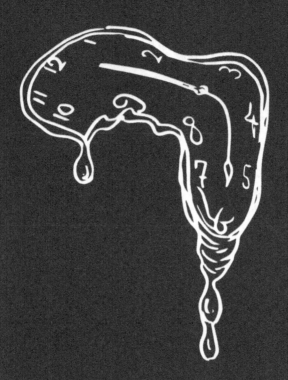

PART THREE

TIMING

1.
TIME
DIFFERENCE

Life expectancy in the UK, Japan, Canada and many other developed nations now exceeds 80 years.

So that means you have about 1,000 months, 4,000 weeks, or 27,000 days to get your stuff done.

If you are 40 years old, you can cut those figures in half.

So you have 500 months left to lead a fulfilling life.

Does that sound like a lot? Or a little?

320,000 hours left. Any better?

38 million minutes. Better?

Once you start hitting the calculator, you'll be less inclined to waste time.

It's precious stuff.

And you will spend a third of that asleep.

You can't be excellent all the time, but you can think about time and how you wish to use it.

80% of employed people and parents feel they are time poor. But research shows we have more leisure time than we did 50 years ago. So why do we feel this way when the facts say otherwise? Nowadays we live in an always-on culture where being busy is seen as a status symbol. We have too much to do and too many distractions. It is simply the perception that we *have* time that makes us happier, whilst the thought that we *don't* have enough time causes us anxiety. So we need to protect our time and use it wisely.

ASK YOURSELF
How can you protect your precious time?

2.
THE CULTURE
OF TIME

In his book, *When Cultures Collide*, Richard Lewis explains how different cultures view time.

Americans regard time as linear.

Time is money and can be divided into clear chunks, each with a price.

Latin people see time as multi-active.

They use a latticework of human interactions to get things done, regardless of specific meetings and timetables, which is why they are often late.

Eastern cultures see time as cyclical.

Everything goes round in a circle.

There are clearly divided views on whether being punctual matters or not.

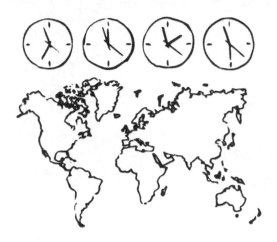

So when considering timing, the first thing to bear in mind is the culture of the person viewing time.

How we want to spend our time will differ for different people, cultures and age groups. The first thing to clarify is how you *want* to spend your time. Our 'Flow State', popularised by positive psychologists Csikszentmihalyi and Nakamura, is a mental state whereby we are fully immersed in an activity and feel energized, focused and joyful. When we're in a flow state, five of our most powerful feelgood chemicals start to surge.[6]

ASK YOURSELF
When are you in flow?

3.
THE FUTURE
IS BEHIND YOU

In the western world, we believe that the past is behind us, and that the future is in front of us.

The Malagasy of Madagascar have a rather different perspective.

They see the future as flowing into their heads from behind them, with the past stretching out in front of them.

According to their world view, the past is visible because it has already happened, which means they can see it.

By contrast, the future is unknown, so it must be behind them, because they can't see it.

To most westerners, this perspective may seem odd.

But in many respects, their view makes a lot more sense than ours.

Time is truly how you choose to see it.

If the past is behind us and future is ahead of us, the result is that the only thing happening right now is the present. You cannot change the past, and you cannot predict the future. So why think about the past and the future when this moment is the only thing that you can control? This is the concept of mindfulness. Mindfulness has been proven to increase positivity and decrease negativity, anxiety and depression.

ASK YOURSELF

When you next catch yourself immersed in future-based and past-based thoughts, can you bring yourself back to the now?

4.
THE YEAR
THAT NEVER IS

The author Douglas Adams
had an interesting perspective
on time. He said:
*"I love deadlines. I love the
whooshing sound they make
as they fly by."*

Many people, and entire companies, wonder why they never seem
to get much done.

Here's why.

In January the year is just getting started. February it's half term.
In March everyone goes skiing.

April has Easter, May has two bank holidays, and in June the schools break up.

In July everyone is on holiday, in August the whole of Europe is shut, and in September people are just getting back into their stride.

October is half term again, in November everyone has flu, and in December they are all in the pub.

That's how the years fly by.

Understanding how time dissipates is the first step towards making good use of it.

Just as business has its own productivity cycles, so do we. In the northern hemisphere we have distinct seasons that affect energy and productivity levels. Summer offers longer days and Vitamin D from the sun, whilst in winter we want to hibernate. More than 1 in 20 people in the UK have been diagnosed with Seasonal Affective Disorder, causing lower mood in the winter months, and therefore less productivity.[7] These energetic peaks and troughs can also be seen every month through women's menstrual cycles.[8]

ASK YOURSELF
Do I understand my own energy cycles?

EVERYTHING
AT ONCE

The eternally wise Albert Einstein taught us:

"The only reason for time is so that everything doesn't happen at once."

Think about it. It's a man-made construct to help us organize things.

You have a choice about how you use time, and how you decide your timing.

But there is a catch.

As Daniel Levitin points out in his book *The Organized Mind:*

"Attention is a limited-capacity resource."

That's why multitasking is a myth.

It doesn't work because there is a switching cost between each task.

We think we are multitasking but in fact we are just flicking between all the jobs and losing even more time.

As Gloria Mark, Professor of Informatics at University of California, Irvine, explains:

"Ten and a half minutes on one project is not enough time to think in-depth about anything."

Do one thing properly. Then move on to the next.

The truth is that we can't do more than one thing at a time. Multitasking is the ability to do a lot of things in quick succession, rather than at the same time. We can, however, quickly switch from one task to another. But the cost of task switching is high, with each switch wasting nearly 1/10th of a second. This can add up to a daily loss of 40% of your overall productivity.[9]

ASK YOURSELF
How can you organise your day so that you focus on one thing at a time?

6.
INPO

INPO stands for 'in no particular order'.

Some people are obsessed with sequence.

Where there is an irrefutable logic, the order in which you do things might well be important.

But sometimes, it just doesn't matter.

As Lao Tzu, the ancient Chinese philosopher and writer, said:
"If you do not change direction, you may end up where you are heading."

Some people are paralyzed by inaction because they don't know where to start.

The cure is to start anywhere.

This applies equally to large volumes of work to do or one single daunting task.

The order doesn't matter, and the timing doesn't matter.

Just get started.

We can give ourselves countless reasons for not starting, or not launching, a project. This is procrastination at its best, which in turn is a form of self-sabotage. *Psychology Today* defines self-sabotage as a self-defeating action that gets in the way of your intent.[10] Perfectionism can be another form of this, preventing us from releasing anything into the world because it 'isn't ready yet'. Drop the excuses and get started. Be prepared to launch something that isn't perfect.

ASK YOURSELF
Can you see this in yourself?

7.
PRECRASTINATION

In his book *#Now*, Max McKeown introduces the concept of Nowists.

Nowists don't worry about the past or the future.

They concentrate solely on positive action now.

They frequently practise what he calls 'precrastination'.

They move the priorities of the future into the present by starting things early.

In fact, unlike those who continually put things off, they actively want to start on new things – the opposite of procrastination.

Even underconfident people can do it.

Author Daniel Levitin calls this 'acting as if'.

If you don't have confidence, you can still act as if you do.

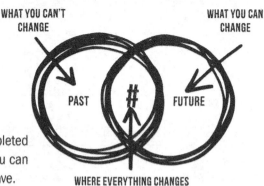

WHAT YOU CAN'T CHANGE

WHAT YOU CAN CHANGE

PAST

\#

FUTURE

WHERE EVERYTHING CHANGES

If you haven't completed a daunting task, you can still act as if you have.

Successful athletes act as if they have already won, by picturing themselves having done so.

Project yourself forward in time and visualize the successful end result.

Visualisation can be a very effective tool. It forces us to think about what it is that we want; if we don't know what we want, we will never get there. It also encourages us to act as if it already exists, allowing the body and mind to prepare and react accordingly to this perceived reality. For this reason manifesting goals is done in the present tense – "I **am** a top goal scorer." The other trick is to be specific, as it will help to paint the picture clearly.

ASK YOURSELF
When can you next practise visualisation?

8.
FORESIGHT/
HINDSIGHT

Some people, as well as companies, institutions and governments, reckon they can foresee what's coming.

They are usually wrong.

Interestingly, the majority of forecasters usually commit two sins.

First, they get their predictions wrong and, second, they get away with it, because no one ever checks whether what they said actually came to pass.

The most accurate prediction you can make is that your prediction will be wrong.

As Sir Humphrey Appleby from the comedy *Yes Minister* wryly observed: ***"I foresee all sorts of unforeseen problems."***

The apparent benefit of hindsight is no more helpful.

We learn very little from history, and yet our desire to pretend that we do leads to a collective blindness about the past.

As Nobel Memorial prizewinner Daniel Kahneman points out:

"Hindsight perpetuates the illusion that the world is understandable."

Hindsight Bias, or the 'I knew it all along' phenomenon, is *'the tendency, upon learning an outcome of an event—such as an experiment, a sporting event, a military decision, or a political election—to overestimate one's ability to have foreseen the outcome'*.[11] The reality is that we rarely foresee things going wrong. We plan as best we can, but we must be realistic - very often things don't turn out that way. Having a plan is great but be comfortable in the knowledge that something else entirely might happen.

ASK YOURSELF
How do you usually react when things don't go to plan?

9.
DON'T WASTE
A CRISIS

"There cannot be a crisis next week. My schedule is already full."

That was the plaintive cry of former US Secretary of State Henry Kissinger as his diary filled up incessantly.

He had run out of time.

Individuals have no control on the timing of events.

What you can control, however, is your attitude to them.

Author Max McKeown believes that a crisis is a terrible thing to waste.

Right-minded people turn an apparent crisis into a decisive turning point that forces a choice between inertia and thinking round problems creatively.

A crisis is not a disaster.

In fact, the stress of one can be the best friend of progress and forward motion.

So, when faced with a crisis you should ask yourself: how can I use this to inspire a new approach?

A *stress response* increases our alertness to deal with the immediate pressure we are facing. Cortisol enables the quick release of glucose, creating immediate energy for our muscles and brain, so that we can act and think quickly. It makes us ready to face the challenge, sharpening our senses and allowing our brain to process information quicker. Whilst we do not want to live in a constant stress state, we cannot avoid stress, and we should not want to, as it is a valuable tool.

ASK YOURSELF
Are you able to appreciate stress for the mini superpower that it is?

10.
POSTCARD FROM
THE FUTURE

If you really want to stretch time forward, try writing yourself
a postcard from the future.

It's a year from now, or ten. Whatever fits your ambition.

Write and tell yourself what has happened.

See if you like it. Then work out what you need to do to make
it happen.

This technique is a bookend to the 'premortem' recommended
by scientist and psychologist Gary Klein.

When an organization has *almost* come to an important decision
but has not formally committed itself, the decision makers gather
for a brief session.

They are asked to imagine that it is one year later and that the
idea has been a complete disaster.

They then have to write a short history of what happened.

The premortem can prevent many a disaster.

By contrast, a postmortem is always too late.

It's all about timing.

By writing a letter from our future selves we are forcing ourselves to contemplate where we want to end up. It makes us think about our own happy ending, what our goals are and what would make us fulfilled. If we don't know where we want to end up, we won't know how to get there. Take some time to visualise where you want to be in the future. Who would you be with? What would you have achieved? What setting are you in?

ASK YOURSELF
What do you want your (happy) ending to be?

HOW TO
CULTIVATE A HEALTHY
MENTALITY

1. Work out how much time you have, and what to do with it

2. Consider other people's views of time

3. Work out your own view on how time works

4. Look at the year and map it out realistically

5. Do one thing properly, then move on to the next

6. If you can't get started, just start anywhere

7. Bring forward some tasks, so that they are done

8. Don't make predictions because they are usually wrong

9. Use a crisis to inspire a new approach

10. Write a postcard from the future to work out where you are heading

PLEDGES

Things you are going to do differently based on the ideas in this section

1. _____

_____

_____

2. _____

_____

_____

3. _____

_____

_____

A WORD ON QUESTIONS

You won't get any helpful answers in life unless you pose some decent questions.

With the possible exception of annoying children harassing their parents, it is almost impossible to ask too many of them.

For a fulfilling and excellent life, it is essential to be relentlessly curious.

Be a mental magpie.

Question everything.

Make sure you truly understand what's going on.

Then, when you are satisfied, you can proceed well informed.

As Richard Feynman, the American theoretical physicist, said:

"I would rather have questions that can't be answered than answers that can't be questioned."

Precisely.

Here are ten of the most powerful.

PART FOUR

QUESTIONS

1.
WHAT'S IT
ALL FOR?

As author John Kay repeatedly asks in his book *Other People's Money*:

"What is it all for?"

It's a fantastic question.

As a man who writes for the *Financial Times*, the subject of his inquiry is usually the money markets and all the extraordinary machinery that goes with it.

But it's a great question to ask of life in general.

So much of what we do is pointless.

A waste of time.

And as we have established, time is precious stuff.

Asking *"What is it all for?"* at the beginning of anything important could save you years of futile effort.

Or even a lifetime of it.

Don't waste your time on things you don't want to do.

Life's too short.

To protect our time, we must learn to say no. So many people are afraid of the word. Maybe you're a people pleaser, afraid of conflict, or don't want to appear prickly. But saying yes all the time drains our energy, pulls us in too many directions, and means we're less likely to do a good job because, if we're honest with ourselves, we didn't want to do it in the first place.

ASK YOURSELF
Next time you don't want to do something, how can you say no?

2.
WHY BOTHER?

Motivation is essential to achieving excellence.

You simply can't get things done without it.

So it is vital to grapple with what at first glance appears to be a somewhat pessimistic question:

"Why bother?"

We need to know, otherwise we have no purpose.

As the business authors Alvesson & Spicer point out in their book *The Stupidity Paradox*:

"We have frequently seen otherwise smart people stop thinking and start doing stupid things. They stop asking questions."

There it is: a lack of inquiry.

Doubtless leading to mindless activity.

And probably to undesirable outcomes.

You have to know *why* you are doing something.

Then you can truly work out *what* you are doing.

In Dr. Rangan Chaterjee's book *Happy Mind, Happy Life*, he explains that one of the three core pillars to achieving real happiness is that of Alignment: what we're doing has to match up with our values. If we are working or living in a way that jars with what we believe in, we will feel uneasy with ourselves. First things first, we need to understand what our values are.

ASK YOURSELF
What are your values, and are you living your life in accordance with them?

3.
IS ANYTHING
REALLY NEW?

Two business school professors called Uzzi and Jones devised an algorithm to analyse a staggering 17.9 million scientific papers to see how original they were.

They discovered that 90% of what was in these 'creative' manuscripts was actually old stuff.

Here's something that all artists know.

It's not where you get it from.

It's where you take it to.

Genius steals.

Or at least adapts and improves.

It's what author Charles Duhigg, in his book *Smarter Faster Better*, calls an intrusion of unusual combinations.

So innovation is effectively 90% known material, with a 10% interesting twist.

Don't start from scratch.

See what's already been done and ask where you can take it to.

Ideas are very rarely original, and the same can be said of the situations we find ourselves in. When going through a tricky patch, it can be comforting to know that we are not the first to go through it, or feel like this. This is not intended to invalidate your feelings, but to remind you that there will be others you can ask for sound advice, a helping hand or to offer inspiration to get you through. This could be someone you know or someone you don't.

ASK YOURSELF
What source could you turn to for guidance?

4.
HOT, COLD
OR SOMEWHERE
IN THE MIDDLE?

In the fable *Goldilocks and the Three Bears* the porridge is too hot, then too cold and finally 'just right'.

'The Goldilocks Principle' has been applied in many walks of life, from cognitive science and developmental psychology through to economics and engineering.

It states that something must fall within certain margins as opposed to reaching extremes.

In other words, it must be 'just right'.

'The Goldilocks Effect' occurs when this blend is perfected.

Far too many people, and businesses, go to extremes.

They either do nothing at all, or disrupt everything.

There's no need. In fact, it's counterproductive.

A little disturbance – not too much, not too little – is the right formula for progress.

Are you doing too much or too little?

In our personal lives, if we do nothing, we are static, unproductive and unhealthy. If we do too much, we will overexert ourselves and head towards burnout. Finding the balance between the two – where we move forward but give ourselves time and space to recharge properly – is how we maintain a productive, healthy and balanced life.

ASK YOURSELF
Are you doing too much or too little?

5.
LOOKING FOR LUCK?

Jack White, musician and founder of *The White Stripes*, believes: ***"Luck is when preparation meets opportunity."***

In other words, if you don't ask any questions, then you certainly won't find any answers.

So you need to prepare.

Preparation can take many forms.

Research. Information gathering. Developing a hypothesis. Testing it with an antithesis. And then arriving at a synthesis.

You have to be a mental magpie.

Be inquisitive and collect thoughts and stimuli.

Then you can join the dots and arrive somewhere interesting when the opportunity arises.

That's not luck. It's inquisition and intelligence finding a home.

As the French enlightenment writer and philosopher Voltaire said:

"Judge a man by his questions rather than his answers."

By asking ourselves questions we are setting up our subconscious and briefing our depth mind. It has been proven that even whilst you are doing something else, your subconscious is still busy working away trying to solve the problem, without you being aware that it is. This is what brings us to those 'aha' moments – when seemingly, out of nowhere, things start to make sense, and the answer arrives.

ASK YOURSELF
Is there a question you should be asking of your subconscious?

6.
WOULD IT HELP?

In the Steven Spielberg film, *Bridge of Spies*, Tom Hanks plays New York lawyer James Donovan.

His mission is to negotiate the release of a US pilot shot down over the Soviet Union in exchange for a convicted KGB spy called Rudolf Abel, played by Mark Rylance.

Three times in the film Rylance asks Hanks the same question.

Hanks: *"You don't seem alarmed."*
Rylance: *"Would it help?"*

Hanks: *"Do you never worry?"*
Rylance: *"Would it help?"*

Hanks: *"You're not worried?"*
Rylance: *"Would it help?"*

It's a superb question.

And, of course, the answer is no, it wouldn't help.

You can be alarmed. You can worry. But it doesn't get you anywhere.

So the next time you are confronted by something vexing and inclined to react emotionally, ask yourself:

"Would it help?"

Worry comes in past, present and future forms. We can stress about what's right in front of us, we can worry about a future event – called *Anticipatory Stress* – or we can ruminate on what has already happened. Or all three at once. If we're not careful, we could be in a state of worry 24/7. Whilst an immediate and short-lived stress response can help us focus, a continual worry state will physically wear us down.

ASK YOURSELF
The next time you are confronted by something vexing and inclined to react emotionally ask yourself: Would it help?

ARE YOU LISTENING?

The biggest communication problem is that we don't listen to understand.

We listen to reply.

We are preparing our next set of remarks while the other person is talking.

As actor John Hurt observed:
"If you listen, you learn; if you talk, you don't."

Interestingly, the word LISTEN contains the same letters as the word SILENT.

Jorge Luis Borges, the Argentine writer, was quite clear on the matter:

"Don't talk unless you can improve the silence."

Wise words.

In a modern context, the philosopher Alain de Botton says:

"True love is a lack of desire to check one's smartphone in another's presence."

We will leave the last word on this to the French author André Gide:

"Everything has already been said, but since no one was listening, we have to start again."

There are two ways to engage in conversation. One is self-centred and ego-based, using the discussion as an opportunity to steer the conversation in a way that works for you, shows off your knowledge, and allows you to dominate. The other is to actively listen and only respond once you have heard and acknowledged the other person, behaving in a way that benefits both parties. One is constructive for just one person, the other for everyone involved. All of us are capable of both.

ASK YOURSELF
Which type of conversationalist are you?

8.
WIBGI?

WIBGI stands for *"Wouldn't it be good if ... ?"*

It's a wonderful, exploratory question, full of possibilities.

Renowned zoologist Paul Meglitsch believes:

"Nearly every great discovery in science has come as a result of providing a new question rather than a new answer."

Think about it.

Yes, of course we need answers.

But there are none without the questions that precede them.

So we need to ask lots of questions. And ask good ones.

We do this naturally as youngsters but, by the time we arrive at work, we have stopped.

According to authors
Alvesson & Spicer:

*"When people are seized
by functional stupidity, they
remain capable of doing the
job, but stop asking searching
questions about their work."*

Wouldn't it be good if we asked more questions?

Asking questions can be beneficial to our career, our
friendships, and our self-worth. By showing interest in a
business contact, colleague or friend, we are giving them
due attention and showing that we care, which often leads to
discovering a shared common ground. There is huge power in
asking a well-timed and pertinent question. By questioning
ourselves we are learning more about our how and why,
opening us up to development and self-understanding. Many
adults with children estimate that about 70-80% of their
children's dialogues were made up of questions. Among the
adults, the estimate was 15-25%.[12, 13]

ASK YOURSELF
Can you ask more questions?

9.
WHAT IS ENOUGH?

Joseph Heller, author of *Catch-22*, and *New Yorker* writer Kurt Vonnegut were at a party at a billionaire's house.

Joseph remarks to Kurt that he has something the billionaire can never have.

"What's that?" asks Kurt.

"The knowledge that I have enough."

It's a hell of an insight.

You have to know when to stop.

It could be a person or a business.

Sometimes, whatever stage you have reached, it's enough.

In an age of relentless forward motion, where it always seems to be more, more, more, it's an interesting question.

What is enough?

Answer that and you'll have the immense satisfaction of knowing when you have indeed arrived at your intended destination.

Our desire for more stems from an age-old time when we needed to compete with others, allowing us to survive in times of scarcity. We needed to be selfish and greedy to stay alive over others. This drive was not designed to make us happy, but rather to survive. Chaterjee calls this the *Want brain*.[14] Whilst the Want brain was developed in the Stone Age, it is now fuelled by a capitalist economy that feeds into the idea that we need more to be successful. But being successful does not equal happiness.

ASK YOURSELF
Next time you reach for more, ask yourself, will it make me happy?

10.
PROBLEM
OR FACT?

We have established that it is important to question everything to ensure that you know why you are doing what you are doing.

But there is a limit.

Sometimes, when you have exhausted every avenue of inquiry, you are better off stopping.

As Shimon Peres, the experienced Israeli politician, pointed out:
"If a problem has no solution, it may not be a problem, but a fact – not to be solved, but to be coped with over time."

Life can be complicated, and you can't solve everything yourself.

In fact, quitting can be winning if it allows you to get on with something more productive or beneficial.

The American economist Alan Greenspan once told an audience:

"If I seem unduly clear to you, you must have misunderstood what I said."

Eventually, you need to stop the questions, understand the facts, and move on.

There is huge power in acceptance. Acceptance allows us to come to terms with the situation we are in, or the event that has passed. It allows us to integrate this experience into who we are, which means that we are working as one, rather than using unnecessary energy battling against ourselves. Sometimes acceptance can lead to a positive reframing of a situation, allowing us to learn and grow. There is a reason that this is the final stage of the grieving process.

ASK YOURSELF
Is there something you can stop dwelling on and learn to accept?

HOW TO
CULTIVATE A HEALTHY
MENTALITY

1. Work out what your life is for

2. Always know why you are doing something

3. Don't always start from scratch – most things have been done before

4. Don't always go for full disruption – a little disturbance might do

5. Prepare inquisitively in anticipation of opportunity

6. Before you do something, ask yourself if it will help

7. Learn to listen properly

8. Sometimes ask: wouldn't it be good if...?

9. Work out what enough is

10. Distinguish between solvable problems and unchangeable facts

PLEDGES

Things you are going to do differently based on the ideas
in this section

1. _____

   _____

   _____

2. _____

   _____

   _____

3. _____

   _____

   _____

A WORD ON DECISIONS

The Latin root of the word 'decision' is *cis* or *cid*.
As in 'scissors' or 'decide'.

Literally, it means to cut off or to kill.

So when you decide, you cut off other possibilities and
go for one thing.

Excellence comes from cutting out the unnecessary.

Many people find this extraordinarily hard to do.

Deciding without thinking is something that only
the most intuitive can do.

For the rest of us, we need to think hard about the choices
we make, and stick to them.

And that includes not wasting time worrying about
what could have been.

'Satisficing' is an elision of to 'satisfy' and 'suffice'.

If it works and it will do the job, then do it.

Now that's a decision.

PART FIVE

DECISIONS

THE UNKNOWN UNKNOWNS

The American politician Donald Rumsfeld made this astute observation:

"There are known knowns. These are things we know that we know.

There are known unknowns. That is to say, there are things that we know we don't know.

But there are also unknown unknowns, things we don't know that we don't know."

The first step to making excellent decisions is to understand what you do and don't know.

This may sound logical enough, but very few people do it effectively.

As St. Jerome wisely pointed out:

"It is worse still to be ignorant of your ignorance."

Awareness of your capabilities and limitations is the place to start.

Finding our blind spots is the first step towards self-development. By working out what we don't know we are able to acknowledge our lack of knowledge. We then have two options – we embrace this with humility, or we decide to learn and fill in the gaps. In yogic philosophy this is called *svadhyaya* or self-study, which requires that we constantly learn to develop and grow as human beings.

ASK YOURSELF
Do you have a knowledge gap that you would like to fill?

2.
NON-PLANNING

Often the best plan is not to have one.

This may sound counterintuitive and, in many respects, it is.

The suggestion is based on two main tenets.

First, too much emphasis on planning usually means that people are surprised when the theory they believed in doesn't happen in practice.

Second, it assumes that the individual is well equipped to make excellent decisions as situations arise, with little forewarning.

This may be a more reasonable possibility than it first seems.

As Jonah Lehrer points out in his book *The Decisive Moment*, we should embrace uncertainty because we know more than we think we do.

You never really know what's coming next.

But you can become adept at adjusting to new developments fast.

Or as boxer Mike Tyson put it: *"Everyone has a plan until they get punched in the mouth."*

We must learn to embrace uncertainty because life is unpredictable. No matter how organised we are, new situations and stimuli will be thrown our way. If we can learn to embrace them, rather than fear them, we will find ourselves far more comfortable with whatever comes across our path.

ASK YOURSELF
Can you find a way to embrace uncertainty?

3.
VAGUE BUT
EXCITING

CERN is the European Council for Nuclear Research, based in Switzerland.

In March 1989, one of their computer scientists, Tim Berners-Lee, submitted a proposal for an information management system to his boss, Mike Sendall.

His response was:

"Vague but exciting."

Tim's idea, of course, went on to become the World Wide Web.

If we are going to make effective decisions, we have to be able to see potential.

In this instance, the vagueness didn't detract from the exciting possibilities.

As authors Chip and Dan Heath point out, to make good decisions you need to widen your options, attain distance before deciding, and prepare to be wrong.

Then test your assumptions.

Or get someone else to if you have a team at your disposal.

Some things are interesting to pursue, if only for fun.

The journey can be as, if not more, valuable than arriving at the destination. It's in the process of attaining your goal that you spend time learning, making mistakes, and indulging in interests. There is value in exploration, in trying things to see what works and what doesn't. You may end up taking a totally different direction to when you set out. The aim of a trek is not just about getting to the end point - it's about the path you take to get there.

ASK YOURSELF
Can you let go of the end result?

4.
ONE THING
ONLY

The processing capacity of the conscious mind is 120 bits per second.

To understand one person speaking to us, we need to process 60 bits of information per second.

Which is why you can barely understand two people talking to you at the same time.

To make sense of all the stimuli thrown at us, millions of neurons are constantly monitoring which aspects of our environment we should focus on.

This is what author Daniel Levitin calls our 'attentional filter'.

Without it, we would be perpetually distracted and bewildered.

Being decisive includes deciding what *not* to do.

As musician Miles Davis pointed out:

"It's not the notes you play, it's the notes you don't play."

For excellence, choose one thing at a time, and decide to give it your full attention.

A vital part of getting your approach right is learning to protect your time and energy. We need our time and energy to focus and do things well. By setting boundaries, we start to put this into practice. Boundaries can be set with friends, families, with work, and with ourselves. The key is to communicate your boundaries clearly, which is not always easy at first, but you will thank yourself in the long run.

ASK YOURSELF
What boundaries do you need to set?

5.
NO PERMISSION REQUIRED

If you have a good idea, then get on and do it.

Don't waste time wondering if it's okay, or waiting to check with someone else.

This is precisely the philosophy of American computer scientist Grace Hopper.

Despite being a United States Navy Rear Admiral, and doubtless being subject to all the etiquette and hierarchy that such an organization demands, her advice was:

"If it's a good idea, go ahead and do it.
It is often easier to ask for forgiveness than it is to get permission."

Yale University recently renamed one of its colleges in her honour.

It takes confidence to enact this degree of decisiveness, but it's worth it.

Making a good decision doesn't need permission, because the quality of the decision speaks for itself.

Rather than permission to start, try getting people's buy-in as you go along. There is huge power in co-creation – working with others. You will have another opinion, different expertise, time patterns and motivation. They will feel invested right from the start. If it's a good idea, people will want to come on the ride with you – they will see the potential and want to get involved.

ASK YOURSELF
Is there someone you could approach to join you?

6.
BE TOMMY COOPER

Here's a classic joke from the comedian Tommy Cooper.

"I said to the doctor, 'It hurts when I do this.'"

Tommy raises his arm.

"He said, 'Well, don't do it then.'"

The logic is irrefutable.

If something doesn't work, or you don't like doing it, then don't do it.

Most people are perfectly intelligent.

And yet they often keep doing the same things again and again without any noticeable improvement in the outcome.

Smart decisions involve identifying what fails to work, and systematically removing those defunct activities.

So if things aren't working, stop doing them.

Decide not to carry on.

Think of something better, and do that instead.

Aparigraha is the concept of non-attachment in yogic teachings. It teaches that we must learn not to cling to possessions and identities because it prevents us from moving freely and accepting the reality that life will change. Our identities and material possessions shift. If we attach ourselves to them, it makes these changes a lot harder to stomach. We will keep ruminating on who we think we should be, what we believe we should own, and try to live up to some sort of expectation. But if we learn to release ourselves from these attachments, and accept the ebbs and flows that life brings, we will be much happier.

ASK YOURSELF
What things or identities are you attached to?

7.
AT WHAT
POINT?

Knowing when to stop is a vital trait.

True behaviour change requires excellent self-awareness and strong discipline.

In the boiling frog anecdote, the premise is that a frog placed in cold water that is gradually heated will not detect the change.

It will allow itself to be boiled to death.

It's actually a myth, because thermoregulation is in fact a vital survival strategy for frogs.

But the metaphor remains helpful for our inability to react to changing circumstances.

If an obese person reaches 20 stone, and then 25, at what point do they think they should take action?

It is important to keep an eye out for things changing around you.

At what point do you say enough is enough?

When you reach that point, make changes to suit the new state of affairs.

Spend some time analysing your current habits. Look at what you do in your day - the cause and effect of what you do based on the day's events. Give each habit a plus or a minus. For example, smoking when you are stressed would be a minus, whereas going for a run because you are stressed is likely to be a plus. Do you have more positives or negatives in your habits? If you need some help on changing your habits, take a look at James Clear's book, *Atomic Habits*.[15]

ASK YOURSELF
How can you shift some of the negative habits?

8.
STRONG OPINIONS
LIGHTLY HELD

If you want to make good decisions, you need to master the art of listening.

Start with a hypothesis.

Look at the antithesis.

Arrive at a synthesis of the two.

Chief Executive A. G. Lafley instituted a new discussion style at Procter & Gamble based on this approach.

It's called 'assertive inquiry'.

It blends advocacy (what I think) with inquiry (what the other person thinks).

That means you have to listen properly – something many people find inordinately difficult to do.

This approach is best summarized in the sentence:

"I have a view worth hearing, but I may be missing something."

This is what Richard Huntington, Chairman and Chief Strategy Officer at Saatchi & Saatchi, calls 'strong opinions lightly held'.

So before you decide on something, ask yourself: what am I missing?

To really hear others, we need to actively listen. The practice of *Active Listening* means that we are actively engaging with what the other is saying, rather than merely being passively present. It is a way of hearing and responding to others that improves mutual understanding. Start by giving your undivided attention to highlight that you believe their voice to be of importance. Defer judgement, provide feedback, and show understanding.

ASK YOURSELF
Can you follow these steps next time you have a conversation?

9.
PING PONG RING

Making decent decisions is really hard if you can't concentrate properly.

You need to remove yourself from distractions to work out what to do.

These days, most of these distractions come from technology.

If only to trick our brains into sticking to a task, we need to organize our time better.

A 'bar code day' is bitty, and subject to continual interruption.

It looks like a bar code because the individual is constantly flitting from one task to another.

In his book *Too Fast To Think*, Chris Lewis references Vanessa Brady, a multi-award winning interior designer.

If two emails have failed to solve a problem, her approach is:

"Ping pong ring."

When the conversation is getting bogged down, break the deadlock with a call.

It has become easy to hide behind technology. By using technology in place of face-to-face conversations, we are removing social interactions from our life. Socialising prevents low mood and can even lead to decreased mortality. Lisa Berkman and Leonard Syme completed a landmark study in 1979 which showed that people with strong social ties were three times less likely to die young than those who were less connected to others.[16] Connecting through real life will sort the problem quicker and offer you a vital dose of social connection.

ASK YOURSELF
When can you next use the phone rather than an email?

STOP TRYING

And finally, remember that quitting can be winning.

Blindly carrying on doesn't always equal success.

Pause to assess what's happening.

As the bishop and social rights activist Desmond Tutu once pointed out:

"There comes a point where we need to just stop pulling people out of the river.

We need to go upstream and find out who's pushing them in."

Sometimes we are simply trying to do the wrong thing.

And you can't do everything.

So, often, the knack is just to stop.

I will leave the last word on this to American actor Robert Mitchum: *"There just isn't any pleasing some people. The trick is to stop trying."*

There is no shame in stopping something or deciding that it doesn't work. By letting go of things and no longer investing our energy in them we allow ourselves to bring in new ideas and give them our full focus. This will motivate and excite us rather than holding us back.

ASK YOURSELF
What can you let go of?

HOW TO CULTIVATE A HEALTHY MENTALITY

1. Work out what you don't know

2. Become adept at coping with new developments – don't over plan

3. Consider some vague but exciting ideas

4. Choose one thing at a time and give it your full attention

5. If you have a good idea, don't ask permission – just get on with it

6. If things aren't working, then stop doing them

7. Work out when enough is enough

8. Have a view, but realize you may be missing something

9. If email isn't solving an issue, pick up the phone

10. Quitting can be winning, so sometimes just stop trying

PLEDGES

Things you are going to do differently based on the ideas in this section

1. _____

_____

_____

2. _____

_____

_____

3. _____

_____

_____

REFERENCES

1. Deloitte study on GenZ https://www2.deloitte.com/content/dam/Deloitte/at/Documents/human-capital/at-gen-z-millennial-survey-2022.pdf

2. The Cost of Interrupted Work: More Speed and Stress, University of California Irvine Study https://www.ics.uci.edu/~gmark/chi08-mark.pdf

3. *The Life-Changing Magic of Tidying*, Marie Kondo (Vermillion, 2014)

4. The Low Mood Loop, *Why Has Nobody Told Me This Before?* Dr. Julie Smith (Michael Joseph, 2022)

5. Forbes 2019 study: Stats: 74 Percent of Americans Prioritize Experiences Over Products. March, 2018. https://www.luxurytraveladvisor.com/running-your-business/stats-74-percent-americans-prioritize-experiences-over-products

6. *Flow*, Csikszentmihalyi, Mihaly (Ingram International, 2008)

7. SAD: https://www.microbizmag.co.uk/seasonal-affective-disorder-statistics/

8. *Wild Power: Discover the Magic of Your Menstrual Cycle and Awaken the Feminine Path to Power*, Pope & Wurlitzer (Hay House, 2017)

9. The True Cost of Multi-Tasking, Susan Weinschenk Ph.D, 2012 https://www.psychologytoday.com/us/blog/brain-wise/201209/the-true-cost-multi-tasking

10. Psychology Today https://www.psychologytoday.com/gb

11. Hindsight bias, first reported by the American psychologist Baruch Fischhoff in 1975

12. Relearning the Art of Asking Questions by Tom Pohlmann and Neethi Mary, 2015. https://hbr.org/2015/03/relearning-the-art-of-asking-questions

13. Why Asking Questions Is Good For Your Brand And Your Career, Goldie Chan, 2021 https://www.forbes.com/sites/goldiechan/2021/02/01/why-asking-questions-is-good-for-your-brand-and-your-career/?sh=204205b91c23

14. *Happy Mind Happy Life*, Dr. Rangan Chaterjee (Penguin Life, 2022)

15. *Atomic Habits*, James Clear (Random House Business, 2018)

16. Social networks, host resistance, and mortality: a nine-year follow-up study of Alameda County residents, Lisa Berkman and Leonard Syme, 1979. https://pubmed.ncbi.nlm.nih.gov/3631060/

BIBLIOGRAPHY

A Beautiful Constraint, Morgan & Barden (Wiley, 2015)

An Optimist's Tour of the Future, Mark Stevenson (Profile, 2012)

Atomic Habits, James Clear (Random House Business, 2018)

Decisive, Chip & Dan Heath (Random House, 2013)

Essentialism, Greg McKeown (Random House, 2014)

Flow, Csikszentmihalyi Mihaly (Ingram International, 2008)

Happy Mind Happy Life, Dr. Rangan Chaterjee (Penguin Life, 2022)

#Now, Max McKeown (Aurum Press, 2016)

Other People's Money, John Kay (Profile, 2015)

Playing To Win, Lafley & Martin (Harvard Business Press, 2013)

Smarter Faster Better, Charles Duhigg (Random House, 2016)

Stuffocation, James Wallman (Penguin Life, 2017)

The Decisive Moment, Jonah Lehrer (Canongate, 2009)

The Empath's Survival Guide, Judith Orloff (Sounds True, 2018)

The Geography of Thought, Richard Nisbett (Nicholas Brealey, 2003)

The Inner Game of Tennis, Tim Gallwey (Pan, 2015)

The Life-Changing Magic Of Tidying, Marie Kondo (Vermillion, 2014)

The Organized Mind, Daniel Levitin (Penguin, 2015)

The Power Of Now, Eckhart Tolle (Yellow Kite, 2001)

The Stupidity Paradox, Alvesson & Spicer (Profile, 2016)

The Subtle Art of Not Giving A F*ck, Mark Manson (Harper One, 2016)

Too Fast To Think, Chris Lewis (Kogan Page, 2016)

Toward A Psychology of Awakening, John Welwood (Shambhala Publications Inc, 2002)

When Cultures Collide, Richard Lewis (Nicholas Brealey, 2005)

Why Has Nobody Told Me This Before? Dr. Julie Smith (Michael Joseph, 2022)

Wild Power: Discover the Magic of Your Menstrual Cycle and Awaken the Feminine Path to Power, Pope & Wurlitzer (Hay House, 2017)

ABOUT THE AUTHORS

KEVIN DUNCAN is a business adviser, marketing expert, motivational speaker and author. After 20 years in advertising and direct marketing, he has spent the last 23 years as an independent troubleshooter, advising companies on how to change their businesses for the better. He also plays guitar.

ROSIE DUNCAN is Kevin's daughter. After an award-winning decade working in media and advertising, she decided to specialise in mental health communications. She now consults some of King's College London's top mental health research centres, working especially with the NHS and military. She also mentors those in the early stages of their career and is the author of *The Early Career Book*.

Contact the authors for advice, training, or speaking opportunities:
kevinduncanexpertadvice@gmail.com
rosieleeduncan@hotmail.com
expertadviceonline.com
theexcellencebook.com

Also by the authors in the Concise Advice series:

The Bullshit-Free Book
The Business Bullshit Book
The Diagrams Book
The Ideas Book
The Early Career Book
The Excellence Book
The Intelligent Work Book
The Smart Strategy Book
The Smart Thinking Book
The Sustainable Business Book

ISBN: 978-1-911687-52-8

ISBN: 978-1-911687-22-1

ISBN: 978-1-911687-53-5

ISBN: 978-1-911671-50-3

ISBN: 978-1-911687-94-8

ISBN: 978-1-910649-85-5

ISBN: 978-1-911687-54-2

ISBN: 978-1-912555-70-3

ISBN: 978-1-911687-96-2